TIFFANY HOPKINS

What He Built from Broken

A Story of Faith, Hope, and Redemption

First published by Tiffany Hopkins 2025

This book was written with the intention of inspiring, uplifting, and encouraging others. The words within these pages are deeply personal and a reflection of my faith journey. If this book has touched your heart, I encourage you to share its message with others while respecting the integrity of the work.

Published by Tiffany Hopkins

Cover Design by Tiffany Hopkins

First edition

This book was professionally typeset on Reedsy.
Find out more at reedsy.com

This book is dedicated to my children—Talon, Duke, and Deacon. You are my world, my greatest blessings, and my reason for everything I do. To my family and those who have shown me true love, your support means everything.

To my sweet angel—my Mamaw Gearl, my Papaw Claymon, Papaw Leonard, and my dear cousin in heaven—I carry your love in my heart always. Your memory gives me strength.

May this book be a testament to faith, love, and resilience.

Contents

Acknowledgments

First and foremost, I give all glory to God. Without His grace, this book would not exist. Every chapter of my life—every high, every low—was held together by His love, His mercy, and His unfailing presence. This is not just my story; it is His story of redemption, woven through my brokenness and rebuilt by His hands.

To my children—thank you for giving me purpose on the hardest days and joy on the best ones. You are my why. Watching you grow has been the greatest honor of my life. You are my heart.

To my parents and family—your steady love has anchored me in ways I didn't always recognize in the moment, but I see it so clearly now. Thank you for your prayers, your sacrifices, and for loving me through every season.

For Mamaw Florene, my aunts, and my cousins Jessica and Stacy— Thank you for being the kind of women who taught me what strength looks like. Your love, prayers, and presence have shaped me in ways words never could. This book carries pieces of you on every page.

To my close friends—thank you for being there when I needed reminding of who I am and Whose I am. Your encouragement helped me keep writing when I wanted to quit.

To those who walked with me during dark chapters and never stopped believing in my healing—this book carries your fingerprints.

To my readers—thank you for picking up these pages. My prayer is that as you read my story, you see traces of your own. And more than anything, I pray you see Jesus—His love, His power to restore, and His ability to make beauty from brokenness.

I

Part One: Brokenness

Psalm 34:18 (NIV) – "The Lord is close to the brokenhearted and saves those who are crushed in spirit."

1

Chapter 1: Freckles, Faith, and the Father's Love

It started with a profile picture.

I was actually having a good day. My hair fell just right, my outfit hit that rare sweet spot between cute and comfortable, and my skin had this glow that wasn't from highlighter—it was just real. I caught a glimpse of myself in the mirror and thought, Okay girl, you did not come to play today. Naturally, I had to capture the moment.

So I snapped a few selfies. Okay... maybe more than a few. After all, good lighting waits for no one. I picked the best one, slapped on a subtle filter, and posted it without overthinking it—mostly.

Then I tossed my phone to the side like I didn't care.

I cared.

Ten minutes later, I was back in the app, pretending I just

happened to be scrolling—but really, I was looking for the comments.

"You're glowing!"

"Absolutely gorgeous!"

"Stop it. You're stunning!!"

And just like that, I felt better. Not healed. Not whole. But... better.

For about 45 seconds.

Then came the spiral.

Would they still say that if they saw me first thing in the morning?

What if they're just being nice?

Why do I need other people to tell me I'm enough for me to believe it?

I'm not proud of it, but I used to let the comment section tell me who I was. On the days I felt invisible in real life, a few fire emojis and a "you're killin' it" felt like a warm blanket. It wasn't love, but it was something. And when you're running on fumes, something feels like everything.

But here's the thing: No amount of "You're beautiful" will fix what's broken on the inside if you don't believe it yourself. I didn't want to be just "pretty" online. I wanted to be known. I wanted someone to see the girl after the picture was taken—the one with leftover pizza in her hair and kids climbing over the back seat—and say, "I still see you."

Confidence wasn't something I just lost. It was something I gave away, one piece at a time—trying to keep the peace, trying to be enough, trying to fit every version of who people thought I should be.

But deep down, I knew God didn't make me to live in pieces.

This isn't a sad story. It's a real one. Full of missed texts, messy kitchens, midnight prayers, and learning—finally—that worth doesn't come from a "like," a relationship, or a good hair day. It comes from being loved by a God who calls you chosen even when you feel like a mess.

I had straightened teeth I spent so much to fix because I didn't see my smile as perfect. I dyed my roots every other week. Kept my nails just right. My lashes were long, but I didn't need all the makeup for God to see me. He didn't need the contour or the highlight. He didn't need me polished.

And when I think about heaven... I don't dream of walking in with a spray tan and a perfectly curated smile. I picture something much more honest. Freckles and pale skin. A crown of messy, red-brown hair and a heart fully seen. I imagine running—barefoot, tear-streaked, joy-soaked—straight into the arms of Jesus. The real me. The one He's always loved.

I don't know about you, but somewhere along the way, I bought into the lie that I had to be everything for everyone. The world doesn't say it outright, but it whispers it loud: Be perfect. Be strong. Be unshakable. And for heaven's sake, don't let them see the cracks.

But here's the truth no one talks about enough: we all have cracks.

Some are hairline fractures we try to ignore. Some run so deep we wonder if they'll ever fully heal. But pain? Pain is the great equalizer. Every single one of us is carrying something. Some drag around grief in oversized duffel bags. Others carry old wounds folded neatly in their pockets. Some burdens are visible. Some are tucked behind polite smiles. But all of us bleed the same.

I've had my days—maybe you've had them too—when I felt like I wasn't doing enough. Not accomplishing enough. Days when a relationship ended and I wondered, What did I do wrong? What part of me wasn't lovable enough to stay for? I've curled up in bed feeling that familiar ache settle into my chest—the kind that whispers, You've been here before. Too many times.

And yet, even in the middle of all that, I never stopped loving deeply. I never stopped giving my best to the people who mattered most—especially my boys.

My three sons were the breath in my lungs. They were my reason to get up, to smile, to keep going. I wanted to give them more than a good life—I wanted to give them my best life. I didn't want them to grow up remembering a mom who just survived. I wanted them to remember a mom who lived. Who laughed loudly. Who prayed boldly. Who wasn't afraid to heal out loud.

For a long time, I thought I had to fix myself before I could come to God. Like He was only interested in the cleaned-up version of me. But that's not who He's after. God doesn't wait for the healing—He meets us in the hurting. He wasn't waiting for perfection. He was waiting for permission. Permission to come close. To sit with me in the mess. To pick up the pieces I thought were too broken to ever be used again.

And oh, how He showed up.

He breathed strength into me when I had none. He lit a fire in me—a holy determination to confront what I'd buried, to speak truth, to rise up from the rubble of old wounds. I was baptized and came out of that water with a fire in my spirit. Not because I had it all figured out—but because I knew He did. And I knew He wasn't finished with me yet.

Every day, I keep stepping forward—not as someone who has it all together, but as someone who has learned to fall into grace. To laugh again. To cry without shame. To mother from a place of wholeness instead of just survival.

So if you're reading this and wondering if it's too late... it's not.
If you're wondering if you'll ever feel joy again... you will.
If you're wondering if God sees you... He does.

And not only does He see you—He knows you. Every crack. Every fear. Every hope still buried under the weight of yesterday. And He calls you worthy.

So if you've ever felt like you're too much and not enough all at once—welcome. You're not broken. You're becoming.

And that's a beautiful place to start.

This isn't just my story—it might be yours, too.

And I pray that in these pages, you won't just find my journey...

You'll find pieces of your own, waiting to be redeemed.

2

Chapter 2: The Lie of Being Chosen

What is it about getting into a relationship and the approval of someone else making you feel like you're now suddenly worthy? What is it about that? I don't get it. Why does someone choosing us somehow make us feel like we're finally enough?

Why do we put the key to our happiness in someone else's pocket—and then panic when they leave with it?

Why do we let their opinion carry more weight than our Creator's?

Why do we bend and break and shrink ourselves to be wanted, hoping that love will mean we're finally whole?

I don't know all the reasons. But I do know the pull—the craving to finally feel like we're enough because someone else decided we were. It's like their approval gives us permission to believe what God has been trying to tell us all along: that we're already loved. Already valuable. Already whole.

But the danger in that? When their love leaves, your worth feels like it goes with it.

I spent so much of my life searching—searching for love, for acceptance, for something that would finally quiet the ache in my chest. Deep down, I just wanted to feel seen. Known. Cherished in a way that would hush the lies I had come to believe about myself.

But no matter where I turned, no matter how hard I tried, I came up empty.

I looked for worth in relationships, convincing myself that if I could just be loved enough—by the right person—I'd finally feel whole. I poured myself into people who never truly saw me. I bent. I shrank. I tried to fit the image I thought would make them stay. And when they didn't, I was left with the same ache. That quiet voice inside that whispered: See? You're not enough.

The truth is, I gave away pieces of myself hoping that somehow, somewhere along the way, I'd feel complete. But the more I gave, the more hollow I became. Love—at least the kind I chased—was fleeting. Conditional. It always seemed just out of reach, no matter how hard I reached for it.

As I moved through my teenage years, that emptiness began to take root in deeper ways. I started recognizing signs of anxiety and depression—though I didn't always have the words for it at the time. I could be in a crowded room, surrounded by people, and still feel completely alone. No matter how much attention I received, or how many friends I had around me, it was like I was on the outside looking in. I laughed. I smiled. I played the part. But inside, I felt lost. Like I didn't truly belong anywhere.

So I kept searching.

I sought worth in approval—shaping myself into what others wanted me to be. I became whoever I needed to be in order to feel accepted. I wore the mask well. I smiled when I was crumbling. I agreed when I wanted to speak up. I showed up polished, even when I felt like I was falling apart.

And yet, the ache remained.

No matter what I did, I always found myself right back in the same place—empty, exhausted, and wondering why nothing ever seemed to be enough. I was chasing validation in places that were never meant to satisfy a soul like mine. And all the while, the one place I truly needed to look was the very place I kept avoiding.

God had been there all along.

But I couldn't see Him—at least not clearly. The noise of my striving, the pressure to be enough, the pain of rejection—all of it blurred my vision. I believed I had to earn my worth, that love was something you won by being good enough. I didn't realize that I had already been chosen. I didn't have to chase it—it had always been mine.

I had spent years trying to fill a God-shaped hole with people, approval, attention, and achievement. But none of it fit. None of it lasted. None of it healed what was hurting.

It took heartbreak. It took failure. It took reaching the end of myself before I finally stopped long enough to listen. And in that stillness, God met me with truth—not condemnation, not disappointment—but grace. The kind of grace that gathers you close even when you feel like a mess. The kind of love that doesn't flinch when you bring your broken pieces to the table.

Looking back now, I see it so clearly.

I was worthy. Not because of what I had done—but because of who He is. My value didn't depend on anyone else's opinion of me. It wasn't rooted in how pretty I looked, how many people liked me, or how perfectly I performed.

My worth was—and always has been—in Him.

And friend, if you're anything like me—if you've ever found yourself worn out from trying to be enough—can I gently remind you of something?

You already are.

You are loved more deeply than you can imagine. Not for the polished version of yourself. Not for the one who gets it all right. But for the real you. The one with fears and flaws and a heart that keeps showing up, even when it feels tired.

The one who has spent so long searching, but was seen all along.

God doesn't love us because we're flawless. He loves us because we're His. And no amount of striving can make Him love you more—and no mistake can make Him love you less.

Would your child making a mistake ever make you stop loving them? Never. Even in their mess-ups, even when they fall short—you don't love them less. If anything, your love leans in deeper. You correct because you care. You guide because you believe in who they are becoming. But your love? It never wavers. It never walks away. It's fierce. Protective. Unconditional.

That's exactly how Jesus loves you.

He doesn't withdraw His love when you get it wrong. He doesn't flinch at your flaws or walk away when you stumble. He draws closer. His heart isn't moved by perfection—it's moved by presence. By your willingness to come to Him, even when you're broken.

The way you love your child through their worst days? Multiply that by infinity—and that's how He loves you. Still. Always. Forever.

I had spent so long trying to earn what was already mine.

But when I finally laid it all down—the masks, the striving, the shame—I discovered something far more beautiful than approval: peace.

I still have my moments. I still wonder if I'll ever feel fully comfortable in my own skin. Will I ever be okay with just being me—unfiltered, undone, and real? I don't know. But here's what I do know: the most important thing has already been settled.

God loves me. And He loves you, too.

That changes everything.

3

Chapter 3: Loud Music, Quiet Pain

For whatever reason, I struggled.

There wasn't a big, dramatic reason I could point to—it was just this lingering feeling of not quite measuring up. Like no matter how well I smiled or laughed or played it cool, something inside me still felt unsure. I tried to act confident, but most of the time I was overthinking everything—how I looked, how I came across, what people thought of me. I didn't know how to say I was insecure, so I just tried to hide it the best I could.

But one thing I never had to hide was how close I was with my sister.

We were only two years apart—she was a senior, I was a sophomore—but we were closer than close. Best friends. Built-in lifelines. She was the one person who saw through the front I put up and loved me exactly as I was. If she was somewhere, you could bet I was right there with her. That was just us.

I don't know how our parents still had a hair on their heads. Honestly, I'm shocked they survived those years. We were double trouble—two teenage girls always together, kind of like sorority sisters who never left each other's side. We were loud. We were wild. We were everywhere, all at once. There wasn't a weekend that went by without plans. And not just one plan—usually several. We were social butterflies with what felt like a hundred friend groups, so between bonfires, ballgames, parties, and late-night food runs, you could be sure we were gonna be there. Wherever there was.

Mornings started in her little black Honda Civic, windows cracked just enough to let in the cool Kentucky air. We'd slide into the seats like we owned the world, crank the volume all the way up, and let the bass rattle the speakers. Whatever was hot on the radio, we sang it like we wrote it. That car was our stage, our vibe, our daily escape. We rolled into school like a scene out of a movie.

We were the fun girls. The cool girls. We'd ride through town picking up our friends, music blaring, feeling like we were in a music video. Low-rise jeans, glossy lips, chunky highlights—we had the trends down to a science. It wasn't about impressing anyone. It was about the energy we brought with us, the freedom we felt, and the way we made every ordinary day feel like something more.

She was the confident one—athletic, magnetic, naturally bold. I always felt a little more unsure of myself, like I was still figuring out who I was. But she never made me feel like I had to keep up. She made space for me. She let me be different without making me feel like I didn't belong.

She included me in everything—plans, friends, laughter, even her closet. We'd get ready together in our room, swapping outfits and stories, putting on makeup, laughing about boys, and making the smallest things feel like the biggest deal.

But isn't it wild how the girl who always seems to be smiling, the one who's the life of the party, can feel the emptiest when no one's looking? Isn't it strange how someone can be so full of energy on the outside... and still be searching for peace on the inside?

It's easy to think that being surrounded by people means you've got it all figured out. But sometimes, the ones who are constantly holding it together for everyone else are the ones who are struggling to hold themselves together. Sometimes the loudest voices are the ones crying out for silence.

We didn't talk about our insecurities or stress—not really. But we didn't have to. We understood each other without needing to say the hard stuff out loud. Our bond ran deeper than words. It was in the way we showed up for each other, no matter what.

Now, when I look back, I don't just see the fun—we had a lot of it. I see the grace that covered us in ways we didn't even realize.

God was there. In the Honda Civic. In the laughter. In the moments that felt silly but somehow held everything together. He was protecting us, guiding us, waiting patiently for the day we'd see just how deeply we were loved.

And when I think about those years now, I don't just see the mess.

I see the music.
  The sisterhood.
  The mercy.

I see two girls doing the best they could to navigate life—and a God who never let them go.

4

Chapter 4: When the World Walked Out, God Stepped In

The crisp mountain air promised another unforgettable night as I slipped into my worn Carhartt coat, the scent of bonfire smoke from past adventures still lingering in the fabric. Laughter echoed through the house as my friends and I hurried to get ready, the thrill of the evening ahead buzzing in the air. But just as we were about to leave, a sudden wave of nausea washed over me, stealing my excitement in an instant. The world around me blurred, my stomach twisting as if warning me that this night would be different from the rest.

My friend looked at me and asked, "Are you okay?"

I shook my head. "No. I feel like I'm going to throw up."

Then, casually, almost as a joke, he asked, "Is there any way you could be pregnant?"

At first, I said no. But then a moment flashed through my mind—

a brief instant that I had blocked out because that guy and I didn't work out. The thought hit me so suddenly, so forcefully, that I couldn't ignore it.

I told them, "You guys go on without me. I'll catch up later."

But what they didn't know was that moments later, I would be calling and confining in a friend to pick up a pregnancy test and meet me at my grandmother's house.

Minutes later, we were sitting on the bathroom floor, cross-legged, staring down at two pink lines.

Positive.

In an instant, everything was different. Just like that—one moment, one heartbeat, and nothing would ever be the same.

I wasn't just a reckless teenager anymore. I wasn't just the girl chasing the next thrill, the next distraction. I was going to be a mother.

And suddenly, everything I thought I knew—about life, about myself, about the future—shifted beneath me.

Once news spread that I was pregnant, everything around me felt different. The calls stopped. The invitations disappeared. My friends kept living life as carefree teenagers, and for the first time, I truly felt what it meant to be alone. The people I once spent every weekend with—the ones I thought would always be there—were nowhere to be found.

I look back now and see how God's hand was in it all. The people who walked away, the paths that were closed off, the plans I thought were ruined—every single moment was leading me here. At the time, it felt like my world was shattering, but in reality, God was stripping away everything that wasn't meant for me so that I could finally see what was.

Because when the world walked out on me, God stepped in.

I didn't deserve His love, but He gave it anyway.

I didn't ask for His grace, but He covered me in it.

I was lost, but He was never lost on me.

II

Part Two: Strength

Isaiah 41:10 (NIV) – "So do not fear, for I am with you; do not be dismayed, for I am your God. I will strengthen you and help you; I will uphold you with my righteous right hand."

5

Chapter 5: A Journey of Growing Hearts

The day my heart grew was the day Talon was born. The moment I laid eyes on Talon, my entire world shifted. He was the most beautiful thing I had ever seen—perfect in every way. His tiny fingers, his soft skin, the way his little chest rose and fell with each breath—I was in complete awe.

As soon as they placed him in my arms, I pressed his delicate face against mine, and in that instant, everything in the world felt right. It was as if time stood still, and nothing else mattered except the overwhelming love I felt for this tiny soul. The weight of him in my arms, the warmth of his skin against mine—it was a love so fierce and all-consuming that I knew, without a doubt, I would do anything for him. I had never loved anything or anyone so much.

I marveled at his innocence, his purity, and the way he instinctively nestled into me, already knowing I was his safe place. Tears welled in my eyes, not out of sadness, but out of a love so deep that words could never do it justice.

From that moment on, I knew my life was no longer just my own. My heart now lived outside of my body, wrapped up in this tiny human who had already changed me in ways I never imagined. I promised him, then and there, that I would always protect him, always fight for him, and always do everything in my power to give him the best life possible.

No matter what life would bring, one thing would remain constant: my love for him was endless, unwavering, and unconditional. That day, I didn't just give birth to my son—I gave birth to a love greater than anything I had ever known.

A few years later, I met the man who would become my husband. He stepped into our lives with open arms, embracing Talon as his own. He also had two boys whom I loved as if they were my own, and Talon cherished them as his brothers. Together, we became a family, bound not just by blood, but by love. We later welcomed another son, Canyon, though we lovingly call him by his middle name, Duke. That day our hearts grew again.

The day my second son was born, my heart expanded in ways I never knew were possible. The moment I saw him, with his beautiful face and a head full of reddish blonde, soft hair, I was completely captivated. He was perfect—a precious gift from God, sent to make our family whole in ways we never even realized we needed.

As I held him in my arms for the first time, I felt that same overwhelming love wash over me, just as it had with my firstborn. But this time, it was different in its own beautiful way. I had already known the deep, unbreakable love of a mother, and yet, here it was again—just as fierce, just as endless, but now multiplied.

He fit into our family so seamlessly, as if he had always been meant to be here. His presence brought a new kind of joy, one that radiated through all of us. Watching his older brother marvel at him with wide-eyed wonder filled my heart to the brim.

From the very beginning, he carried a light within him, a sweetness that filled every room and every heart. He was a reminder that love is limitless, that our hearts always have room to grow, and that the most beautiful blessings come wrapped in the tiniest packages. My precious boy, the one who made our love grow even deeper—he was everything I never knew I needed, and more.

I never imagined my heart could expand the way it did, but the love I felt for my boys was boundless, equal, and unwavering.

Mental illness made it incredibly hard for me to stay constant in how I felt in my marriage at that time. My emotions were often unpredictable, swinging from happiness to sadness. That instability played a huge role in the emptiness I carried. It wasn't that I didn't love my family—I loved them deeply—but my mind made it nearly impossible to feel settled.

After several years, I left my marriage, searching for whatever it was I thought I was missing. In that search, I entered another relationship, hoping to find the missing piece of myself. But even there, the emptiness remained.

I truly gave that relationship all I had at the time—which, looking back, wasn't much despite trying so hard. I was grieving so deeply over my grandpa during that season, barely holding myself together most days. I was trying to be well, trying to be whole, trying to be everything I thought I needed to be. But I was pouring from a heart that was cracked and tired, still learning how to heal while carrying the weight of too much loss.

Thirteen days after leaving that relationship, I found out I was pregnant again. Not long after, I returned to the only life I had truly known—back to my ex-husband. Though we were no longer married, he stepped in to take me to doctor's appointments, to be present when I needed him, and to help me raise my youngest son—our son we had together—and my oldest son. He stepped up for us all.

The day Deacon was born, I fell in love again. From the moment I laid eyes on him—his soft blonde hair, his bright blue eyes that held the depth of a thousand unspoken words—I knew he was meant to be mine. He was breathtaking, a little piece of heaven wrapped up in my arms.

Little did I know, this tiny baby in my arms would grow to be my feisty one—full of life, full of fire, and full of laughter. He would be my country boy, the one who found joy in the simple things, who loved being goofy and making others laugh. He could make everyone around him laugh with his quick wit and mischievous grin.

His brothers were in awe of him, just as I was. Watching them gently reach out to touch his tiny fingers, seeing their eyes light up with wonder and love—it was a moment that would be etched in my heart forever. He wasn't just my baby; he was their baby too. The one they would protect, laugh with, and love fiercely for the rest of their lives.

He was my little light, my unexpected but perfectly placed blessing. I thanked God for him with every breath, knowing that He had once again filled my life with a love so deep, so pure, that words could never fully capture.

For the first year of Deacon's life, my ex-husband stood by me, ensuring I was not alone in navigating motherhood once again.

I will always be grateful that, despite everything, I had someone to share life's experiences with, someone to navigate the challenges of parenthood alongside me. It was a gift to have a partner in raising my boys—even one who was not their biological father. The love he gave them—the way he stood by them—was something I will never forget.

I've come to see that within every struggle, there is an unseen battle of the heart—a constant, quiet war between hope and despair. Looking back, I realize how difficult it must have been for my ex-husband to love someone who didn't yet know how to fully receive or accept love. Loving someone with mental illness can feel like an emotional storm—unpredictable, exhausting, and, at times, overwhelming. If not managed properly, it can take a toll on everyone involved. Looking back, I don't think I had the tools to be in a healthy relationship, let alone at such a young age. I was still maturing, struggling with major depression and anxiety, and lacked the emotional bandwidth to be the kind of wife that marriage required.

Despite all my silent struggles, I was extremely loving, deeply affectionate, and always seeking to feel needed and important to someone. I poured myself into being a devoted wife—keeping the house clean, trying to be everything my partner needed.

We fought for years to hold it together, but in the end, we came to the painful yet necessary realization that sometimes the greatest act of love is knowing when to let go. And so, with grace, we chose to walk away. We respect each other immensely and show that respect to each other always.

But what nobody ever talks about is how hard it is to walk away from someone else's children—the ones you loved like your own. You try to hold on to them as much as possible from afar because you love them and always will. The ones whose baby teeth all fell out while you were there. The ones whose fingernails you clipped and hairs you helped fix. The ones you went on family vacations with. The ones you celebrated birthdays and Christmases and Thanksgivings and Easters with. Those rooms you decorated and cleaned so they would be so perfect for them. The ones whose rooms you go sit in and catch up on life with them about everything because it was important because they were important to you.

There's a grief that comes with losing the life you built. The shared routines. The inside jokes. The way you knew each other's thoughts without speaking. Your ex wasn't just someone you loved—they were your best friend. Your partner. The person you grew up with, built dreams with, weathered storms with.

And now, suddenly, they're just... gone.

Relearning how to live again is the hardest part. Relearning how to breathe without their presence in the room. Relearning how to smile without feeling guilty. Relearning how to fill your days when the life you knew no longer fits.

It's not just heartbreak. It's a kind of mourning. For the kids. For the love. For the version of yourself that only existed in that life.

And still—somehow—you keep going. You find a new rhythm. You carry them in your heart, even if not in your arms. You learn to live in the quiet. You learn to grow again, even if it's with a limp.

What we chose in the end was growth over resentment, peace over bitterness, and family over ego. It would've been easy to let pride take over, to walk away bitter or to hold onto blame. But we didn't. We chose what was best for the kids. We chose grace. We chose to honor the good, even when it was wrapped in hard things. Because no matter what came between us, we both loved our children more than we loved being right. And that kind of love—the kind that puts healing before pride—is what holds a family together, even when the shape of that family changes.

But I didn't stay in that place of emptiness. I knew I wanted more—for myself and for my children. I wanted to be the healthiest, happiest version of the woman God created me to be. So I made the brave choice to go to therapy, and it changed everything. I began to learn how to manage the highs and lows that once felt so overwhelming. I discovered tools that helped me regulate my emotions, find clarity in the chaos, and take back control of my life. It wasn't always easy, but every step forward was a reminder that healing is possible. I fought hard to grow, to heal, and to become the kind of mother, woman, and believer I knew I could be. And I'm proud of that fight—because it led me to a version of myself that is strong, steady, and full of hope. A version of me who could be truly present—really present—for my children, and strong enough to make beautiful things happen without being dependent on others to carry me.

Years have passed, and he is happy now—and that is what I want for him more than anything in this world. We both grew through our pain and found clarity in the pieces that were left behind. We came to understand that we were better as friends, and that kind of peace doesn't come easily. The things we walked through—together and apart—shaped us into who we are today. I genuinely prayed for him to find the kind of love that heals, even if it couldn't come from me. And I believe he's found it. A love he is absolutely deserving of. A love that brings him comfort, laughter, and steadiness.

And just as importantly, our children—all of our children—are deserving of that kind of love, too.

She makes them feel loved. Really loved. Seen, known, and cared for in ways that matter. She makes room for all of them, including my oldest, who isn't biologically his—but who has always been his in every way that counts. And she treats him as her own, with a kind of tenderness that I could never thank her enough for.

She loves them with such grace and goodness. She doesn't have to—but she chooses to—and that kind of love is sacred. It's what I always hoped for them. And in the process, she became someone I didn't know my heart needed. A friend. A constant. Someone who sees my love for them and never questions it. Someone who cheers me on as I cheer for them. She understands me without needing explanations. She just gets it.

She is the safe place I didn't expect to find in this chapter of life—and I love her for it, more than words can say.

And Deacon would be the first child his father ever had. Their bond runs deep. The love they share is undeniable. He has been surrounded by love on all sides, and I can see now how God was working behind the scenes the whole time. Even when it didn't look how I thought it would, He was piecing it all together

"For I know the plans I have for you," declares the Lord, "plans to prosper you and not to harm you, plans to give you hope and a future." (Jeremiah 29:11)

6

Chapter 6: Embracing God's Strength

I poured out my heart in prayer, cried in the quiet, and let Him into the places I had tried to fill with people. He met me there—not with judgment, but with mercy. Not with shame, but with comfort.

He reminded me that even when love fails, He never does. When people walk away, He stays. When my heart breaks, He's the one who mends it.

And I'm learning—slowly, sometimes painfully—that healing doesn't always look like getting back what you lost. Sometimes, it's about becoming someone new in the process. Someone stronger. Someone softer. Someone who finally knows her worth.

"So do not fear, for I am with you; do not be dismayed, for I am your God. I will strengthen you and help you; I will uphold you with my righteous right hand." – Isaiah 41:10

I truly sensed His gentle voice urging me to draw closer—to trust Him and leave my old ways behind. I chose not to resist. Within days, I felt an overwhelming closeness to Him, sharing my thoughts and feelings freely, and placing all my faith in His promise to work everything out for the good of me and my boys, even amid chaos. I was reassured that He had a plan for my life—a plan that transcended all my pain.

So many signs began to unfold, affirming that I was on the right path. One day, as I walked down the street, a neighbor I'd never spoken to stopped me and said, "I told my wife that I needed to invite you to church the next time I saw you." In that moment, I realized that my longing to be among fellow believers was not just a desire—it was a divine appointment.

"Trust in the LORD with all your heart and lean not on your own understanding; in all your ways submit to Him, and He will make your paths straight." – Proverbs 3:5-6

Another pivotal moment arrived when I posted online, inviting friends to join me for walks. To my amazement, a devoted family member reached out, eager to join me. Little did I know then how close we would become. She turned out to be my confidant, my church buddy, and someone who lovingly shared the Word of God with me. Her presence reminded me of the promise that when two or more are gathered in His name, He is in their midst. Time and again, as we delved into Scripture, I felt the Holy Spirit move within me—electrifying every hair on my arms and igniting a passion for God I had long thought lost.

Recognizing the need to move forward, I made the conscious

decision to cut ties with anyone who hindered my progress, and a profound peace enveloped me as I embraced this new chapter of my life—one devoted entirely to drawing closer to God.

One morning, while attending church with my friend, the opportunity for baptism arose. My heart pounded with anticipation and a touch of fear. My knees began to buckle under the weight of the moment. Turning to her, I whispered, "Sis, I have to go now. Will you go with me?" Without hesitation, she took my hand and led me to the front.

I confided in someone there, saying, "I can't do this without my son, who is supposed to be here today." My oldest child, who had been searching for me throughout the service, came forward when the church announced that if he was present, he should join me at the front. As he approached, tears streamed down his face, and in that frozen moment, we embraced. We cried together, and then he stood by my side in the water as I was baptized.

Words cannot fully capture the beauty of that day—especially since just five days prior, my remarkable 16-year-old son had given his life to the Lord. We were both baptized in the same church, a testament to God's amazing grace. I cherish a photograph from that day—a tangible reminder of our glorious moment, surrounded by fellow believers, my dear friend by my side, and my mother celebrating with us.

In my lowest moments, I learned to lean wholly on God's strength. His promises carried me through the darkness, guiding me toward a future filled with hope and renewal. Let these words remind you that even when our hearts are broken, God's love is more powerful than anything we face.

7

Chapter 7: Stepping into a New Season

I want to share a moment when God revealed Himself in a way that I will never forget. After taking my son to the doctor, I stopped by McDonald's for a quick bite. In that ordinary moment, an unexpected call from a lady at the bank changed everything. She asked if I was interested in one of their products—a question that, under normal circumstances, would have filled me with hesitation. But something within me stirred, urging me to visit the bank.

With my son's meal still warm in my hands, I made my way to the bank. As I spoke with her, a thought lit up inside me: "Why not explore the possibility of getting approved for a home loan for me and my boys?" Despite my doubts—thinking I might not even qualify for a loaf of bread—it felt like a divine invitation. The lady eagerly took down my details and assured me she would connect me with their loan officer.

To my astonishment, the loan officer called the very next day. His support was incredible; despite the hurdles we encountered, his confidence and determination shone through. I had braced myself for rejection, yet every door seemed to swing open effortlessly—doors that no one could shut.

What many don't know is that a few months before that day, I had taken a quiet moment to write down the desires of my heart. I envisioned a lovely white home—my sanctuary, solely in my name, for me and my boys. I dreamed of returning to college, of earning my degree, and of stepping boldly into a future I had long only dared to imagine.

From the moment I saw that home online—even though it wasn't perfect—something in my heart whispered, "This is the one." I knew in my soul that I had to take my children with me. My choice had to be something that they would all embrace; I wouldn't be at peace with any other option. The first time I viewed the home alone, I felt an indescribable connection. Later, when I brought my boys with me, the moment they walked through the door, they echoed my silent conviction: "This is it." I had kept my initial impression to myself, not wanting to influence their pure, untainted feelings about the place. I was moving to a new city where I had no family or friends—only the clear, unwavering direction God had placed on my heart. It wasn't far from where we had lived before, but it was a new start—a leap of faith that I had to take for the sake of our future.

Today, I stand as a living testament to God's love and mercy. I closed on and purchased that white home I once dreamed of, accepted the bank's offer for one of their products, and I'm back in college—excelling and well on my way to earning my degree. Along this journey, I have forged relationships with those who believed in my vision, and I have joyfully shared my testimony, hoping that even one soul might be drawn closer to Him.

Nothing is too big for God. I could not have accomplished any of this without His grace. The precise timing and miraculous unfolding of events are clear reminders that it could only be God at work. I have strived to obey Him and deepen my relationship with Him, and in return, He has cared for my family in ways I never thought possible.

It's essential to remember to glorify God not only for the blessings we see but also for the protective measures we may not fully understand. His hand is in every twist and turn of our journey, and I am eternally grateful for His guidance and mercy.

One profound way to cultivate humility and gratitude is by consciously acknowledging the goodness in everyday moments. Consider the simple joys: having enough coffee to brew a comforting cup, possessing just enough money to treat yourself, savoring a warm meal or indulging in your favorite dish, and even having sufficient gas to reach your destination. These seemingly insignificant details hold great meaning, reminding us that every blessing is a manifestation of God's favor.

8

Chapter 8: Walking in His Light: A Faith Renewed

In the wake of all my heartbreak and hardship, a new chapter began—one marked not by what I had lost, but by what I had found in God's unwavering love. I realized that every tear, every moment of doubt, and every struggle had led me to this point of renewal. I began to see that even in the darkest valleys, His light was there, guiding me toward a future filled with hope.

Every day, as I embraced my new reality, I learned to trust more deeply in His plan. I found that when I surrendered my worries and my past, I could walk in the light of His promise. With every sunrise, I was reminded that His mercies were new every morning. In the quiet moments of prayer and reflection, I heard His gentle voice urging me to step forward—one small, courageous step at a time.

I started to establish routines that anchored me in His truth: moments of quiet reflection with Scripture, heartfelt conversations with those who shared my journey of faith, and daily acts of gratitude for even the simplest of blessings. I learned that true transformation doesn't happen overnight; it grows slowly, nurtured by trust, persistence, and the gentle guidance of the Holy Spirit.

One particularly transformative day, as I sat with my boys in our new home, I looked around at the life we had built together—a life I once thought impossible. The laughter of my children, the warmth of our shared moments, and the steady rhythm of our everyday routine became a living testament to God's love. I understood that every trial, every heartbreak, was a stepping stone leading me to a deeper, more intimate relationship with Him.

I began to see that walking in His light meant embracing not just the victories, but also the struggles, knowing that each challenge was an opportunity for growth. I learned to lean on His strength when my own was insufficient, to find comfort in His promises when the world felt too heavy to bear. His Word became my compass, and His presence, the constant reassurance that I was never alone.

I started to share this journey with others—speaking openly about the struggles, the heartbreak, and the miraculous ways God had intervened. Whether through a kind word, a shared prayer, or a simple act of kindness, I wanted others to know that no matter how deep the pain, there was a light waiting to guide them out of the darkness.

Through it all, I discovered that true renewal is not about forgetting the past; it's about learning from it, allowing it to refine us, and then choosing to walk boldly into the future with faith as our guide. I realized that I was no longer defined by my scars or the mistakes I had made. Instead, I was defined by the transformative power of God's love—a love that continues to renew my spirit each day.

"Your word is a lamp for my feet, a light on my path." – Psalm 119:105

Now, as I walk in His light, I stand as a living testament to the truth that no matter how dark the night, His love is brighter. I am renewed, I am hopeful, and I am determined to continue this journey with a heart full of faith, knowing that His promises will carry me forward into a future that is as brilliant as it is certain.

9

Chapter 9: When God Holds Your Heart

God is not far away from your pain—He's right there, closer than your breath, holding you even as you cry.

Think of the shortest verse in Scripture: "Jesus wept." (John 11:35). Jesus stood at the tomb of his dear friend Lazarus, surrounded by Mary and Martha's grief, and He wept. He knew He was about to raise Lazarus from the dead, yet He still paused to share in the sorrow of that moment. Why? Because God's heart is moved by our pain. If Jesus could weep with His friends, you can trust that He is weeping with you too, catching each tear. In fact, one psalmist beautifully wrote that God collects all our tears in His bottle (Psalm 56:8), as if each tear is precious to Him. Not one drop of your heartache is unnoticed by your Heavenly Father.

So, dear friend, even in this season of deep hurt, you are not abandoned. "Never will I leave you; never will I forsake you," God promises (Hebrews 13:5). When you feel most alone, whisper His name—Jesus. In the stillness, you may sense that

He's sitting beside you on the bed or in the car as you drive aimlessly to clear your head. He is Immanuel, God with us, even now—especially now. Let that truth be a soft place to rest. You can pour out every feeling to Him—the confusion, the anger, the despair—and know that He listens with compassion. "The Lord is a refuge for the oppressed, a stronghold in times of trouble." (Psalm 9:9). There is no need to hide your pain from God; He welcomes the real you, tear-stained and honest.

As you recognize His nearness, allow yourself to be cradled by His presence. Just as a loving friend wraps you in a hug while you sob, God's Spirit wraps around your broken heart with comfort. You might not feel that comfort immediately—sometimes the ache is so deep it's hard to feel anything else. But faith isn't a feeling; it's a trust that God is holding you even when feelings say otherwise. Picture yourself held in the safety of God's hands, even as you feel broken. He will not let you be destroyed by this. "The Lord is near to those who have a broken heart" (Psalm 34:18), and because He is near, you will not be consumed by the sorrow. In the middle of the night, when the loneliness presses in, remind yourself in a gentle whisper: He's here with me. He's not going anywhere.

Grace for Your Regrets

Heartbreak has a way of making us replay every regret on an endless loop. "If only I had been better... If only I hadn't said those words... How could I have missed the warning signs? Why did I give my heart away so easily?" These questions and self-accusations crash over you, compounding the pain with guilt and shame. But listen closely: God doesn't want you living under that burden of self-condemnation. There is grace for every mistake, every sin, every "if only" that haunts you.

You are not meant to carry the weight of regret forever. Jesus carried all our failures to the cross so we wouldn't have to carry them in our hearts. Scripture assures us, "There is now no condemnation for those who are in Christ Jesus" (Romans 8:1). No condemnation means that through Jesus, you are forgiven and set free. God is not blaming you repeatedly—so you don't have to keep blaming yourself.

God longs to restore you, not punish you. "I, I am He who blots out your transgressions for my own sake, and I will not remember your sins." (Isaiah 43:25). If God chooses not to remember your past mistakes, you can choose not to endlessly rehearse them either.

Let grace speak louder than shame. Take a moment in prayer, name your regrets, and place them into Jesus' hands. He already paid for them. Hear Him whisper, "You are forgiven. You are still precious. This is not the end of your story."

You are redeemed, beloved, and free.

Surrendering the Pain

Now, having acknowledged your pain and released your regrets, there comes a holy invitation: surrender.

Surrender doesn't mean pretending you're fine. It means handing over to God what's too heavy to carry alone. Picture yourself removing the heavy backpack of heartbreak, anger, and disappointment. Jesus stands before you and says, "Let me carry that for you."

"Come to me, all you who are weary and burdened, and I will give you rest." (Matthew 11:28)

That verse is more than comfort—it's a lifeline. You don't have to be strong. Your strength was never the requirement—His was.

Surrender might look like praying, "God, I can't carry this anymore." Or crying in His presence and letting yourself fall apart safely. Or journaling out every fear and then saying, "Lord, I trust You with this too."

It's not a one-time act. Some days, you'll take your pain back. That's okay. Just come again. God understands.

There is beauty in surrender, even when it's messy.

The Quiet, Sacred Work of Healing

Healing is often invisible at first. Like a wound healing beneath a bandage, it happens slowly—layer by layer. Don't despise small steps: the morning you laugh, the afternoon you breathe deeper, the night you finally sleep through.

"He who began a good work in you will carry it on to completion." (Philippians 1:6)

Some days will still hurt. Some memories may sting. But that doesn't mean you're not healing. It means you're human. Be gentle with yourself.

Rest. Walk. Journal. Listen to worship music. Sit still. These are not small things—they're sacred tools of recovery. And if needed, talk to someone—a friend, a pastor, a counselor. God often sends healing through others.

And when you feel like you're slipping backwards, remember this: Setbacks do not erase progress. You are still healing. Especially when it hurts. That's when the deepest work is often happening.

A New Dawn

"Weeping may last through the night, but joy comes with the morning." (Psalm 30:5)

Heartbreak can feel like endless night, but joy is coming. Slowly. Softly. Surely.

God will bring beauty from ashes. "He will give a crown of beauty instead of ashes, the oil of joy instead of mourning..." (Isaiah 61:3)

What feels like wasted years can be restored. "I will restore to you the years the locusts have eaten." (Joel 2:25)

God is rebuilding you. Brick by brick. Hope by hope. He's not just restoring what was lost—He's preparing something better. Something new. Something that fits the heart He's healing within you.

Dare to believe that love is still ahead of you. Dreams are still ahead. Joy is still ahead.

Let this be your whisper in the darkness: "The morning is coming. And God is with me until it does."

10

Chapter 10: God Made a Way

There comes a time when the impossible suddenly becomes possible—a moment when you look back in awe and realize that every barrier was shattered by God's grace. For me, that moment arrived in a cascade of breakthroughs that transformed everything.

As a single woman, I stepped boldly into a future I once thought unreachable. I purchased a car in my name for the very first time—a symbol of independence and the freedom to chart my own path. It wasn't merely a vehicle; it was a tangible reminder that God was paving the way, breaking through the limitations of my past, and setting me on a course toward a brighter future.

Not long after, another dream became reality. I purchased a home in my name—a sanctuary for me and my boys, a place where our laughter and love could flourish. Every brick, every door, and every window spoke of new beginnings. I moved to a new city, away from the familiar confines of my old life, guided solely by the whisper of God's calling.

And as if that weren't enough, God blessed us even further. I was able to purchase my oldest son his very first car—a milestone that filled him with pride and marked his first steps toward independence. In those moments, gratitude overwhelmed me. It wasn't just about the cars or the house; it was the undeniable truth that God made a way when I had almost lost hope.

Each of these achievements was not the result of my own strength, but a testament to His love and provision. They were signs that I was on the right path—a journey of obedience, trust, and relentless faith. Every time I turned a key, walked through a door, or handed over the keys to my son's first car, I was reminded that nothing is too big for God.

I gave Glory to God for every detail of our journey. I shared my testimony, eager for others to know that even when the road seemed impossible, God's hand was at work, opening doors that no one could shut.

11

Chapter 11: The Battle Within

There were moments when I felt it creeping in—this slow, subtle drift away from God. It wasn't always obvious at first, but I knew. I could feel it in the depths of my soul. The moments when I wasn't drawing closer to Him, I was undoubtedly drifting away.

Spiritual warfare is real. It's not just something you read about in Scripture—it's something you feel, something you battle, something that tries to wrap itself around you like a shadow. And I was in it.

There were days when I found myself pulled toward worldly distractions, letting my attention shift away from the One who had saved me. I didn't even realize it immediately, but the signs were there. I wasn't praying like I once did. I wasn't seeking Him with the same fire. I wasn't feeling the overwhelming presence of the Holy Spirit the way I once had. And that absence? It was unbearable.

I had tasted true peace—the kind only God can give. And now, I felt its loss in every ounce of my being.

Without Him, I was restless. Unsettled. The world offered temporary satisfaction, but it was never enough. Nothing was the same without Him. No success, no possession, no earthly pleasure could fill the void that only He could. And I knew—I had to get back.

So I cried out, just as I had before: "Lord, I need You. I don't want to live a single day without You. Draw me back to You."

And He did.

Because that's who He is—a God who never truly lets go, even when we wander. A Father who stands with open arms, ready to embrace His child the moment they turn back.

But I also learned that God places people in our lives as reminders of His presence, as pillars of faith to lean on when we are weak. And for me, that person was my amazing friend, Catrina.

Anytime I felt myself slipping, anytime I sensed that distance creeping in between me and God, I longed to be near her. She was strong in her faith—so deeply rooted in His Word that just being around her made me want to draw closer to Him.

I held onto the promise of Matthew 18:20: "For where two or three gather in my name, there am I with them." And I knew that when I was with Catrina, we weren't just talking—we were gathering in His name.

We had Bible study over the phone, reading Scripture and encouraging each other in the Word. We walked the track together, our conversations filled with gratitude and praise. Every interaction, every moment spent with her, pointed me back to Him.

She reminded me to read my Bible, to stay consistent with my daily devotions, and to keep my heart fixed on God, no matter what distractions tried to pull me away. I am beyond thankful for her—for our friendship, our sisterhood in Christ, and the way she constantly uplifted me in faith.

On the morning of my baptism, it was Catrina whom I turned to. I felt the Holy Spirit stirring inside me, my heart pounding as I realized—this was the moment. I turned to her and whispered, "I know it's time."

Without hesitation, she took my hand and led me to the front of the church. She praised God as I stepped forward in faith, ready to surrender my life completely to Him. She was right there with me, standing beside me during one of the most sacred and transformative moments of my life.

She had been such a big part of my journey, pushing me closer to God, encouraging me, and walking this path of faith with me. And on that day, she stood with me again—witnessing the moment that I fully gave my life to Christ.

Through her, I saw another example of God's love—a reminder that we don't have to fight our battles alone. He gives us people to walk with, to lift us up, and to help carry us back to Him when we start to drift.

I had learned a powerful truth: Life without God is no life at all. And I never wanted to be apart from Him again.

III

Part Three: Hope

Romans 15:13 (NIV) – "May the God of hope fill you with all joy and peace as you trust in him, so that you may overflow with hope by the power of the Holy Spirit."

12

Chapter 12: The Pieces I Lost

There are moments in life that shape us, not just by what we gain but by what we lose. Loss has a way of etching itself into the deepest corners of our hearts, leaving behind an ache that never fully fades. And for me, some of the deepest wounds came from losing the people who had loved me the most—the ones whose presence had been steady, unwavering, and full of a kind of love I had never known anywhere else.

My grandparents were everything to me. Their love was pure, unconditional, and constant in a world that often felt uncertain. They had the kind of love that was rare, the kind that withstood time and trials—a love I admired and longed for but never quite found for myself. They were my safe place, my foundation.

And then, piece by piece, I lost them.

Cancer took them both just a few years apart, and with them, it felt like parts of me went, too. The grief was unbearable. I had been so close to them my entire life that when they were gone, I didn't know how to move forward. It wasn't just the loss of their presence; it was the loss of the love they poured into me—the kind of love that made me feel truly seen, truly cherished.

I never wanted to feel that kind of pain again. Losing them shattered me in a way I couldn't comprehend, and I subconsciously built walls around my heart, fearing that if I ever loved someone that deeply again, I would only be setting myself up for that same unbearable heartbreak.

But my losses didn't end there.

Before I lost those two, I had already experienced unexpected loss. My Grandfather, who was amazing and that I loved, gone too soon.
And then my cousin passed. Someone who I could always turn to, someone who understood me in a way few others ever could.

He and I could laugh until we cried, talk about anything, and find comfort in each other in a way that made life feel a little lighter. And just hours before God took him home, we had spoken. The weight of that still sits heavy on my heart.

Grief became a familiar shadow in my life. And the way I coped? I didn't. At least, not right away.

I avoided it for as long as I could. I placed the pain on a shelf, trying to walk away from it, pretending I was fine. I thought if I ignored it long enough, maybe it wouldn't break me any further. But grief doesn't work that way. It waits. It lingers. It surfaces when you least expect it—sometimes months, sometimes years later—demanding to be felt, demanding to be dealt with.

And when it finally caught up to me, it was overwhelming.

I can't talk about the woman I have become without talking about the loss and heartbreak that shaped me. Each piece of pain, each goodbye, each empty space left behind—it all played a role in who I am today.

But through it all, even in the moments when I didn't know how I would go on, God was there. He held me through the tears I refused to cry. He waited patiently as I tried to outrun my grief. And when I finally turned to Him, when I finally let myself feel the weight of it all, He was right there, ready to carry it with me.

I still miss them. I always will. Some wounds never fully heal, but they change us. And in that change, we find the strength to keep going.

Some days, I have the capacity to sit with my memories, to smile through the tears, and to feel the warmth of their love even in their absence. But some days, I just don't have the heart or the mental strength to face it. Some days, it's just too hard. The pain doesn't go away—it lingers, it aches, it resurfaces when I least expect it.

Grief is love with nowhere to go, and my love for them will never fade. But neither will my faith in the God who continues to carry me through it.

13

Chapter 13: The People God Placed

In life's intricate design, a support system serves as a lifeline—woven delicately through every joy, every heartbreak, and every chapter in between. Above all, we find our unwavering strength in God. But closely following are the people He places in our path—those sacred souls who speak the language of our hearts without words, who offer their presence through every mountaintop and valley. Their love is quiet but fierce, simple yet profound. And their presence is a reminder of God's goodness made visible through human hands.

Among those God has placed in my life, my mother has always been my constant. She's my hero. She's the steady place I run to when the world feels unsteady. She's the one who taught me what it means to love with your whole heart, how to raise children with both pride and tenderness, and how to choose what's right, even when it's hard.

She knows every part of me—every flaw, every secret, every scar. She's seen the sides of me I tried to hide, the pieces I felt ashamed of. And yet, her love never wavered. She's loved me through it all.

My son Talon has grown into an extraordinary young man—athletic, faithful, and wise beyond his years. But I know I couldn't have raised him alone. Life was full. There were practices and school events I couldn't always attend, moments I couldn't always catch. But my mom and dad stood in the gap. They showed up, loved him fiercely, and helped me shape him into the young man he is today.

My mom is fierce. A protector. A fighter. She's taught me to speak up and stand strong for my children. She pushed me forward when I felt like I couldn't even crawl. When I was worn down and weary, she breathed life into me. I thank God every day for her. I don't know how I could face a world without her in it.

I've laughed until I cried with my mom more times than I can count. The kind of laughter that sneaks up on you, doubling you over, wiping tears from your face while she's still sitting there straight-faced like she didn't just deliver the funniest line of the night. She's hilarious without even trying—and somehow, those are always the best kinds of people.

She's the person I want beside me when I'm not doing good. When I just need someone to sit next to me on the porch at night, under a blanket, with my head on her shoulder and the weight of the world slowly falling off my chest. She's the one I begged to stay all night with me because—no matter how old you get—you're never too old to want your mom.

She's the one I call when everything feels like it's falling apart—but nine times out of ten, she ends up making me mad before I feel any better. She doesn't sugarcoat anything. She'll hit me with the truth like it's a friendly suggestion, all calm and matter-of-fact, while I sit there trying not to argue. But then I can't help but laugh, because deep down, I know she's right. She always is. It's just her way—love you hard, tell it like it is, and then ask what we're gonna eat.

And in the circle God built around me, there's my Aunt Shelia. Though she's technically my aunt, our bond feels more like sisters. We've shared laughs, loss, memories, and healing. From late-night talks and road trips to comfort food and spontaneous adventures, she's shown up time and time again. Her love is a covering, her presence a peace I didn't know I needed.

Then there's my ex-husband's mother Minnie. The love we share is deep and forever. She's been a second mother to me—not because she had to be, but because she chose to be. Her love for Duke, and her acceptance of all my children, has been one of the most precious gifts of my life. She's poured herself into our lives with a grace that reflects the very heart of God.

My sister has been a built-in best friend—my anchor in the highs and lows of life. She's laughed with me, cried with me, stood with me. She's held my hand through joy and pain and reminded me who I am when I forgot.

My cousins have shown up in moments when life felt impossible—helping me pack and unpack, physically and emotionally. They've stood with me through transitions, cheered me on, and carried the weight when I couldn't hold it alone.

To my aunts, nieces, and nephew—you are my tribe. The kind of people who don't come and go with the wind but plant themselves beside you and weather every storm. You've taught me about loyalty, grace, and what it means to truly show up for someone.

These people—this chosen, hand-picked circle—have been God's provision for me. They've reminded me that we were never meant to do life alone. They are proof that even when our prayers are silent, God is listening. That love, real love, doesn't always shout—it shows up. It stays. It holds on.

So to anyone out there who's still finding their circle—don't give up. Pray for your people. Pay attention to who shows up. Let go of the ones who don't. There is no shame in walking away from what drains you so you can hold close what sustains you.

God gives us people not just to comfort us—but to reflect His love back to us.

"Two are better than one, because they have a good return for their labor: If either of them falls down, one can help the other up." —Ecclesiastes 4:9–10 (NIV)

14

Chapter 14: Love Beyond Words: A Mother's Journey with Duke

From a young age, my heart held a tenderness I didn't fully understand. I remember being just a little girl when I saw a child with special needs and quietly whispered a prayer: "God, if it's Your will, bless me with a child like this to love." While other kids were dreaming of adventures and toys, I was asking God for something different—a deeper kind of love, the kind that required presence, patience, and purpose.

Years later, that quiet prayer would take shape in the form of my son, Duke. I began noticing signs of autism when he was around 18 months old. It wasn't something that came with a clear road map. The journey to a diagnosis was filled with questions, evaluations, waiting lists, and advocating when I felt exhausted—but I never once considered giving up. Duke is, without a doubt, one of the greatest joys in our lives.

He doesn't just bring light into a room—he is the light. Every little thing he does is filled with such sincerity. His heart is gentle, his love is pure, and his presence is grounding. There's nothing performative about him—what you see is real, honest, and deeply beautiful.

Duke's love for his Nanny is especially powerful. He counts down the days until he sees her again, and if too many pass without a visit, he starts to worry. His mind becomes consumed with thoughts of her, wanting to know that she's okay, that she's happy. Their bond is more than just special—it's sacred. When they're together, there's this unspoken connection between them, like their hearts are wired to the same rhythm. It's a bond that fills our home with warmth and reminds us what love across generations is meant to look like.

Duke feels everything deeply. If you're kind to him, even in a small way, it matters. It sticks with him. Sometimes it even moves him to tears. He teaches us to slow down, to appreciate the little things, to recognize love in all its quiet, beautiful forms.

God knew what my heart needed when He gave me Duke. Being a mom of a child who is autistic hasn't just changed my life; it's expanded my soul.

I will always be in his corner. Always fighting for him, always celebrating him, always making sure he is seen, heard, and treated with the dignity he deserves. He is more than enough—he is perfectly placed in our family, just the way God intended.

And as I look back over our journey, I'm reminded of the promise in Romans 8:28:

"And we know that all things work together for good to them

that love God, to them who are the called according to His purpose."

God's plan for Duke—and for me—was never a mistake. Even in the challenges, He's been working, shaping a story that is full of grace, growth, and immeasurable love.

And as I reflect on our journey, I see purpose. I see the fingerprints of a loving God who knew exactly what He was doing when He chose me to be Duke's mom. What once felt uncertain has become sacred. Every moment—every challenge, every joy—has drawn me closer to the heart of God and shown me a love that is wide, deep, and beautifully intentional.

15

Chapter 15: Embers of Renewal: A Quiet Redemption

One of the most meaningful transformations in my life has been in my relationship with my dad. For many years, we weren't close in the way I had hoped. There was love there, but it wasn't always easy to find or express. Our connection was more quiet, more distant, and for a long time, I carried an ache for something deeper. Still, through the years, time and grace began to soften what once felt unchangeable.

There was something magic about the way my dad and I would come alive to music. No one else seemed to understand it like we did. When nobody else wanted to jam, we were there, cranking up the tunes as loud as the speakers could handle. The coffee was always black, just the way we liked it, and we'd belt out lyrics to songs like "Tina at the Teardrop Inn" by Fastlane.

The song's words hit us hard, and there we were, sitting on the porch in the light of the sun, caught up in the rhythm. My dad's foot tapping to the beat, his eyes closed like he was feeling every note, and me, my knee slapping in time with the music, in the zone with him, completely connected. We didn't need anything else but each other and the song.

We could've listened to music for hours and never gotten tired of it, always saying, "Listen to this one." The way each song came alive in the speakers, like a treasure we were sharing, was pure magic.

One of my absolute favorites was "Simon Crutchfield's Grave" by Nothin' Fancy. We'd play it over and over, interpreting the lyrics our own way. It was our own little inside thing, a moment of deep connection in the music.

And the thing was, it wasn't just the music. It was the way we vibed together. We were so similar. Personality and all.

I remember giving him a small figure of Jesus—just a simple gesture, hoping it would speak to his heart. With sincerity, I told him, "God loves you and is always with you." He looked at it, a bit unsure of what to say. It wasn't rejection—it was unfamiliar territory. He simply didn't know how to receive it. And that was okay. In that moment, I realized he was still on his journey, just like I had been on mine.

Even so, I carried a quiet hope that through my life and love, he might come to feel God's presence in his own way. I had seen the power of transformation in my own life, and I trusted that God could reach him too—gently, patiently, and in His perfect timing.

Some time later, I found another gift I felt led to send. I ordered it and had it delivered to his house, addressed to him. Funny enough, I forgot all about it after I ordered it. But God didn't forget. One crisp morning, I stopped by for coffee, and as I pulled in, a postal worker was handing him a package. The timing couldn't have been more perfect—almost like God Himself had scheduled that moment.

His eyes lit up with curiosity as he opened it. When he saw what was inside, a smile tugged at the corners of his mouth. He looked over at me, genuinely touched, and said, "Thank you—I really love this." Then, after a small pause, like it had been sitting on his heart, he added, "Hey, I've still got that baby Jesus you gave me. It's sitting on my dash so I can see it every day." My heart swelled. That simple moment spoke volumes.

No grand speech. No dramatic shift. Just a quiet opening of the heart, a small sign of connection, and a reminder that love and faith can grow even in unexpected soil.

Maybe my dad is stronger in his faith than I've ever given him credit for, and maybe even stronger than I am in my faith. Maybe it just looks different than mine. I don't know the quiet prayers he's whispered or the private moments he's had with God. I don't know the ways he's wrestled or the strength it's taken for him to keep going. And the truth is, I'm not meant to know all of that. I'm not the judge of another person's walk with the Lord—only God is. What I do know is this: God sees the heart. And that's all that truly matters.

As the years have gone by, I've seen a side of my dad I treasure deeply. He has become the most incredible grandfather. He and my mother never miss a game. He takes such an interest in everything the kids are doing. He helps with school drop-offs and practice pickups alongside her, giving their very all as the very best. On their birthdays, he goes online and finds birthday songs with their names in them, playing them loud enough to fill the house with laughter and dancing. He brings joy effortlessly, making us laugh until we cry. At Christmas, he shops online for me all on his own for a heartfelt gift, without needing suggestions—just quietly making me feel remembered and cherished. That all speaks volumes about the love that lives in his heart.

I now see how he gave of himself over and over without asking for anything in return. I don't remember him ever doing much for himself. He always put us first.

And now that I'm a parent myself, I can finally see how hard this role is. And in the moments when I couldn't be there for my kids—he was. The very man I once longed for a closer relationship with stepped into the gap. That's grace. That's redemption. The quiet kind that changes everything.

I wonder if my dad ever realized he helped carry me through my divorce—and through the quiet, consuming battle with an eating disorder that followed. Not with long talks or emotional advice, but in the quiet, unspoken way only he could. We'd sit out in his building, listening to Lynyrd Skynyrd, or some bluegrass band like Lonesome River Band or IIIrd Tyme Out, and we'd just be. No pressure to talk. No expectations. Just the hum of music crackling from the speakers and the comfort of each other's company.

There was something healing in the way he'd tap his barefoot on the floor, how he'd nod with his eyes half-closed when the harmony hit just right. I'd sit in the chair across from him, letting the sound fill all the spaces where words had failed me. That building became our sacred space—where silence didn't feel empty, it felt safe.

We didn't need words. His presence told me everything I needed to hear.

God doesn't require perfection from any of us—only a heart that's willing to love and grow. And my dad's heart has always been bigger than I realized. I love him for who he is, and for how far he's come. And more than that, I've come to see—he's always loved me, too.

"May the God of hope fill you with all joy and peace as you trust in him, so that you may overflow with hope by the power of the Holy Spirit."
—Romans 15:13 (NIV)

16

Chapter 16: Finding Joy in the Journey

Not every moment in my life has been heavy with sadness. Though loss and heartache have shaped me, they do not define me. My story is also filled with light—laughter that made my stomach hurt, memories that I hold close to my heart, and the kind of love that reminds me of God's goodness every single day.

My boys have brought me immeasurable joy. They are my greatest blessings, my deepest love, and the reason I push forward with everything I have. With them, I have laughed until I cried, danced around the house, and created a home filled with love, warmth, and memories that I will cherish forever.

And then there are my friends—the ones who have stood by my side through every season. With them, I've had the kind of conversations that last until the early morning hours, the kind of laughter that heals wounds I didn't even know I had, and the kind of love that reminds me that true friendship is one of life's greatest gifts.

I have lived.

I have loved deeply and with all my heart and soul.

I have made wonderful memories with the people who matter most to me.

But through all of it—the highs and the lows—I have learned that some things are simply not meant for me, and that's okay. I've had to let go of certain people, certain dreams, and certain versions of myself that no longer served who God was calling me to be. Letting go hasn't always been easy, but it has always been necessary. And each time I have walked away from something or someone that wasn't meant for me, I have found more of myself.

I have tried to be a person that others can count on. Someone who holds space for the people in my life, who listens with an open heart, who shows up when it matters most. Integrity has always meant everything to me—I want to be solid, unwavering, and true to who I am, no matter what life throws my way.

Through it all, I've found that I am happiest when I keep my circle small. My family—those who have loved me unconditionally—are my safe place. They are the ones I can be my most authentic self with, the ones who have seen me at my best and my worst and still love me the same.

I know this: I am who I am for a reason. I am uniquely made by God, and there is no one else like me in this world—just as there is no one else like you.

And so, I find beauty in who I am, even though I am not perfect.

Because I was never meant to be perfect. I was meant to be His.

I spent so much of my life fighting—fighting for love, for acceptance, for control over things that were never mine to hold. I fought against the pain, against the memories, against the gnawing emptiness inside me that no amount of distraction could fill. I carried the weight of my past, dragging it behind me as if I could somehow make sense of it all if I just held on long enough.

The truth is, my hands were never meant to carry those burdens.

There comes a moment in life when you reach the end of yourself. You try and try to hold everything together, but no matter how strong you think you are, the weight becomes too much. I remember that moment for me—the breaking point where I had nothing left to give, no more strength to pretend I had it all under control.

I had spent years trying to prove myself, believing that if I worked hard enough, if I tried a little more, I could fix everything. I could make up for the mistakes, for the broken relationships, for the feelings of unworthiness that had chased me since childhood. I thought I had to be strong, that I had to keep fighting. But what I didn't realize was that true strength doesn't come from holding on—it comes from letting go.

Surrender.

That word used to terrify me. To surrender meant to admit defeat, to give up control, to let go of the illusion that I could do it all on my own. But what I've learned is that surrender isn't weakness—it's the greatest act of faith.

When I finally fell to my knees, exhausted and broken, and told God, "I can't do this anymore," something shifted. I expected to feel ashamed, to feel like a failure. But instead, I felt peace.

For the first time, I wasn't carrying everything alone.

God had been waiting for me to let go. He had been there all along, watching me struggle, waiting for me to stop trying to fight battles that weren't mine to fight. And the moment I surrendered, He stepped in.

Looking back, I see how He was orchestrating everything—the pain, the losses, the closed doors. I thought I was being abandoned, but He was actually protecting me. He was stripping away everything that wasn't meant for me so that I could finally see what was.

When I let go, I made room for Him to move.

I started to see that I didn't have to earn His love. I didn't have to prove my worth. He had loved me all along—through every mistake, through every bad decision, through every tear I cried alone in the dark.

Surrender wasn't about giving up—it was about finally stepping into the life God had been calling me to all along.

Because the moment I stopped trying to control everything, God began to heal what I had been desperately holding together.

He turned my brokenness into beauty.

He turned my struggles into strength.

And He turned my hopelessness into a story of redemption.

"I waited patiently for the Lord; He turned to me and heard my cry. He lifted me out of the slimy pit, out of the mud and mire; He set my feet on a rock and gave me a firm place to stand."
— Psalm 40:1-2 (NIV)

17

Chapter 17: The Porch, the River, and the Promise

Dream so big it makes people pause—not because they doubt you, but because they've never seen courage like yours before.

Set your sights on something so bold, so wildly full of faith, that it stretches beyond what others are used to seeing. Let them tilt their heads in curiosity—not because they think you're lost, but because something about your vision stirs something in them they've forgotten how to reach for.

Because here's the truth: those who chase extraordinary things rarely start with applause. They begin with whispers of doubt all around them—and still choose to take the first step.

Why?

Because they aren't held hostage by fear or the need for validation.

They don't wait for the stars to align.

They don't tiptoe around the question, "But what will people think?"

They move.
They dare.
They believe.

I've always been drawn to that kind of boldness. The kind that doesn't wait for permission. The kind that listens when God calls, even if no one else understands.

And I've learned something beautiful: even when the world doesn't see your worth right away, God always does.

When I first said things like,
"I think I'm going to write a book,"
"I think I'm going to go back to school,"
or "I think I'll buy a house,"—
some smiled with polite nods, unsure of what to make of my dreams. Others gave me genuine encouragement that lit a fire in my heart. Their belief became a quiet strength I could lean on when mine felt shaky.

There were also moments when the support didn't run as deep as the smile. But I don't carry resentment. I carry grace. Because I've learned that not everyone can see what God has shown you—and that's okay.

What matters most is that I kept going.

Because here's what they didn't see: my dreams weren't rooted in applause or validation. They were rooted in faith. And even when my journey didn't fit the world's mold, I knew who was guiding my steps.

Mental illness was a part of my story—but it never defined

my ability, my intelligence, or my calling. I don't glorify the struggle, but I do honor the strength it built in me. I've become deeply observant. Intuitive. Brave. I don't just hear people—I see them. I read what's unspoken. I understand what it means to fight quietly and love deeply.

And I've had people—beautiful, compassionate, faith-filled people—who clapped for me with their whole hearts. People who didn't just say "I believe in you," but meant it. Who saw the woman I was becoming and stood beside me with joy. Their support was God's reminder that I was never alone.

I remember saying one day, "Maybe I'll be a New York Times best-selling author." And not everyone believed—but some did. And even if I never make that list, I've already reached something far greater: the hearts of those who needed hope.

Because sometimes, the biggest win isn't fame—it's faithfulness.

This book you're holding? It was written on the porch of the house I prayed for—the one by the river I dreamed of. The house God gave me in His perfect timing. I said it. I believed it. And He delivered. That's not luck. That's promise.

I've walked through seasons where I felt invisible. Where life was more about surviving than thriving. But I've also walked into answered prayers that reminded me of who I am and whose I am.

So I don't tell you all this for pity—I tell you because there is power in perseverance. And there's purpose in your pain, too.

If you're battling mental illness, I want you to hear this loud and clear:

You are not broken.
You are not weak.
You are not disqualified.

You are capable. You are worthy. You are loved.

God doesn't reserve dreams for the most polished or put-together. He uses the willing, the faithful, the ones who move when He says "go"—even if their voice trembles.

And even if the world never claps, He does.

So clap for others. Celebrate with joy. Let your wins be a light, not a comparison. And never stop cheering for yourself, too.

Because healing is beautiful. Growth is holy. And dreams—especially the ones planted by God—are always worth chasing.

And today, I can say this with peace in my soul:

I didn't just survive—I soared.

Not by the world's power, but by the grace of a God who never gave up on me.

I began writing more, a passion that has always been deep in my soul, something that came naturally to me and really helped me express what I was going through. I began walking, which also added to the pace I felt and was something I needed to do to be in motion and active. I also started taking up yoga and pilates here and there, really doing things that I needed to do just for me. I learned more about my own journey. It became clear that self-care wasn't just a luxury—it was a necessity for me. I started journaling my thoughts and feelings, writing about things I'd never been able to voice before. Whether it was going for early morning runs or setting aside time to write, I was actively rebuilding my life, finding joy in the little things. I'm in college full-time, thriving in that aspect of my life. Obtaining my degree was something on my bucket list, a personal goal I wanted to achieve. Being a full-time student also became a source of pride for me—it wasn't just about the grades, but about proving to myself that I could accomplish something I set out to do. Completing assignments and mastering new concepts filled me with purpose. God has really worked in me, and it's all a reminder that, even when life gets tough, growth is possible.

Philippians 1:6 (NIV)

"Being confident of this, that he who began a good work in you will carry it on to completion until the day of Christ Jesus."

18

Chapter 18: Made for More

I am creative.
I am compassionate.
I am resilient.
I am joyful.
I am capable.
I am worthy.

I am exactly who God knew I would be when He knit me together in my mother's womb.

And I haven't even scratched the surface of all He's going to do through me.

There are things I've accomplished on my own—things I never dreamed were possible.

I've walked through doors that only opened because I dared to believe.

I've faced battles no one saw and came out stronger than I ever thought I could be.

Not because I had it all together—but because I refused to give up.

So now I ask you...

What's in your heart that you've been afraid to reach for?

What dream keeps tugging at you, no matter how many times you try to silence it?

What if the very thing you think disqualifies you is exactly what God wants to use?

Here's the truth:

You don't have to stay small just because the world made you feel like you should.

You don't have to dim your light to make others comfortable.

If God placed a dream in your heart, it's not by accident. It's a seed—and seeds don't look like much in the beginning.

But give them faith, give them time, give them light, and they'll grow into something beautiful.

You can do hard things. You already have.

You can rise above the pain, the doubt, the fear.

You can push through with everything you've got—and when you do, you'll leave others wondering how you made it.

And when they ask, you can smile and say, "It wasn't me. It was God."

You'll lead them to hope. You'll lead them to faith.

Because your story won't just be about survival—it'll be about transformation.

I've learned that I don't need a partner to feel whole.

I've found purpose that doesn't depend on being chosen by someone else.

I'm steadier now. Stronger.

More confident in who I am and what I bring to the world.

I'm driven by something deeper—by calling, by peace, by the quiet strength God placed inside me.

I am living proof that God can use a willing heart, even one that's been through the fire.

That He can build beauty from brokenness.

That He honors the woman who keeps showing up, even when it's hard.

You are not too late. You are not too broken.

You are not forgotten, overlooked, or unworthy.

You are becoming.

So take the step. Say the prayer. Write the dream down.

Because what God is doing in you is bigger than what's behind you.

This is just the beginning—and I'm ready for all of it.

Here's to the beauty ahead, and the God who walks with us through every page.

I'm no longer just surviving—I'm living, becoming, and believing.

I was made for more.
And the best part?

He's not done yet.

19

Chapter 19: Beauty from Brokenness

To the One Who's Still Trying to Trust Again

You don't have to pretend.
Not with me. And not with God.

Maybe you're tired of being strong.
Maybe you're carrying the weight of things no one ever apologized for.
Maybe you're still piecing yourself together from moments that shattered you quietly.

I want you to know something—there's no shame in that.
There's no shame in needing time. In needing grace. In needing God more than ever.

You don't have to be fixed to be found faithful.
You don't have to be fearless to be used.
You don't have to have it all figured out to still be right in the center of God's will.

He's not looking for your perfection. He's after your heart.

The raw, cracked-open, desperate-for-hope kind of heart.

"A broken and contrite heart, O God, You will not despise." (Psalm 51:17)

So if today you feel like you're starting over again...

If all you've got is a mustard seed of faith and a half-whispered prayer—

That's enough.

You are not weak for needing grace.

You are not broken beyond repair.

You are not forgotten in the waiting.

"He will restore the years the locusts have eaten." (Joel 2:25)

That means even the years that feel like a blur... even the ones you spent lost, angry, numb, or ashamed.

He can redeem every moment.

And He will.

So don't rush this chapter.

Don't compare your process to someone else's progress.

Don't think you're behind just because your journey looks different.

You're healing.

You're growing.

You're being made new from the inside out.

And healing isn't loud or showy—it's quiet. It's holy.

It's choosing to believe that God's love still applies to you, even here.

So if no one else says it today: I'm proud of you.

Not for being perfect, but for still showing up. For still trying.

For choosing hope even when it scares you.

That matters.

You matter.

You never really know when God is using you.

You may feel ordinary, overlooked, or still too broken to be of any use—but someone is watching.

Someone is drawing strength from your survival.

Someone is finding hope in the way you keep showing up.

Even when you don't realize it, your story is speaking.

Every scar, every tear, every prayer you've whispered in the dark—none of it is wasted.

God is weaving it all into a testimony that will touch lives you may never even meet.

Because sometimes, the very thing you thought disqualified you is what God uses to set someone else free.

"They overcame by the blood of the Lamb and by the word of their testimony." (Revelation 12:11)

Keep going.

You have no idea how many people are watching you walk through fire—and finding faith that they can walk through theirs, too.

A Prayer for the One Who's Still Trying to Trust Again

God,

You know exactly where this one is. You know the questions they're afraid to say out loud.

You know the weight of the wounds they carry. And You love them right here.

Thank You for being the kind of God who draws near to the brokenhearted.

Remind them that they don't have to fix themselves to be loved by You.

Help them release the lies they've believed about their worth.

Help them rest. Breathe. Heal.

Walk them gently out of the fear that has tried to own them.

Speak peace over every anxious thought.

Speak life into every place that has felt numb or dead inside.

You are not done with their story.

You are not finished with their heart.

In Jesus' name,

Amen.

IV

A Message from My Heart

My greatest hope is that through my story, others will see the undeniable goodness of God. I pray that they will recognize His power to transform even the most broken pieces of a life into something beautiful and whole. He is the One who can strip away the desires that lead us astray and replace them with a fulfillment so deep, so unshakable, that nothing in this world can compare. Through Christ, we are made new—strengthened, refined, and given the courage to face any challenge.

Love,
Tiffany

About the Author

Tiffany Hopkins is a devoted mother of three boys. She grew up on a holler called Greasy Creek in Eastern Kentucky. Her sons are her world—the driving force behind everything she does. Their love and laughter inspire her daily, pushing her to be the best version of herself.

Tiffany finds peace in writing and has a deep passion for sharing the love of Jesus Christ with others. Through her words, she hopes to uplift and encourage those navigating their own journeys of faith, healing, and redemption. She also strives to bring awareness to mental illness, advocating for understanding, compassion, and the importance of seeking help.

She treasures the simple joys in life—being at home with her children, creating lasting memories, and embracing the beauty of everyday moments. Her faith is the cornerstone of her life, guiding her through challenges and filling her heart with gratitude. She firmly believes that no matter how broken the past may be, God can create something truly beautiful from it.

Made in the USA
Columbia, SC
04 June 2025